AMANTES ASSEMBLE

Abhijit Naskar is the 21st century Neuroscientist and Poet who has been serving at the forefront of humankind's struggle against sectarianism. As an untiring advocate of mental health and global harmony, he became a beloved best-selling author across the world with his very first book "The Art of Neuroscience in Everything". With his revolutionary contributions in Cognitive and Behavioral Neuroscience Naskar has helped the world tackle the horrors of systemic racism, biases, hate, extremism, discrimination and stereotypes more effectively, because of which he is lovingly hailed by humankind as 'the humanitarian scientist'.

AMANTES ASSEMBLE

100 Sonnets of Servant Sultans

ABHIJIT NASKAR

Also by Abhijit Naskar

Lives to Serve Before I Sleep
When Humans Unite: Making A World Without Borders
All For Acceptance
Monk Meets World
Mission Reality
Citizens of Peace: Beyond The Savagery of Sovereignty
Operation Justice: To Make A Society That Needs No Law
See No Gender
The Gospel of Technology
Every Generation Needs Caretakers: The Gospel of
Patriotism
Aşkanjali: The Sufi Sermon
Mad About Humans: World Maker's Almanac
Revolution Indomable
When Call The People: My World My Responsibility
No Foreigner Only Family
Hurricane Humans: Give me accountability, I'll give you
peace
Ain't Enough to Look Human
Servitude is Sanctitude
Time To End Democracy: The Meritocratic Manifesto
I Vicdansaadet Speaking: No Rest Till The World is Lifted
Boldly Comes Justice: Sentient not Silent
Good Scientist: When Science and Service Combine
Sleepless for Society
Neden Türk: The Gospel of Secularism
Martyr Meets World: To Solve The Hard Problem of
Inhumanity
The Shape of A Human: Our America Their America
When Veins Ignite: Either Integration or Degradation
Heart Force One: Need No Gun to Defend Society
Solo Standing on Guard: Life Before Law
Generation Corazon: Nationalism is Terrorism
Mucize Insan: When The World is Family
Hometown Human: To Live For Soil and Society
Girl Over God: The Novel (Abi Naskar Adventures Book 1)
Gente Mente Adelante: Prejudice Conquered is World
Conquered
Earthquakin' Egalitarian: I Die Everyday So Your Children
Can Live
Giants in Jeans: 100 Sonnets of United Earth
Vatican Virus: The Forbidden Fiction (Abi Naskar
Adventures Book 2)
Karadeniz Chronicle: The Novel (Abi Naskar Adventures

Book 3)
Şehit Sevda Society: Even in Death I Shall Live
Handcrafted Humanity: 100 Sonnets For A Blunderful
World
Mücadele Muhabbet: Gospel of An Unarmed Soldier
Making Britain Civilized: How to Gain Readmission to The
Human Race
Dervish Advaitam: Gospel of Sacred Feminines and Holy
Fathers
Honor He Wrote: 100 Sonnets For Humans Not Vegetables
The Gentalist: There's No Social Work, Only Family Work
Either Reformist or Terrorist: If You Are Terror I Am Your
Grandfather
Woman Over World: The Novel (Abi Naskar Adventures
Book 4)
High Voltage Habib: Gospel of Undoctrination
Bulldozer on Duty
Find A Cause Outside Yourself: Sermon of Sustainability
Ingan Impossible: Handbook of Hatebusting
Amor Apocalypse: Canım Sana İhtiyacım

DEDICATION

To the reformers who remain sleepless for society,
so that the rest of humanity can sleep.

CONTENTS

1. Actual Holy Trinity (Sonnet 1)

Sonnet 1

Holy Trinity
(The Sonnet)

Civilization is founded on 3 pillars,
Conscience, courage and compassion.
Without these three there is no society,
Only a prehistoric mockery of civilization.
When all three come together, lo and behold,
Here rises the holy trinity - the holy trident!
You can use it to plough the land of creation,
Or use it to devour the divisions most obstinate.
Wasting precious lifeforce chanting like a parrot,
Do not go chasing fiction out in the wilderness.
Wipe the rust off your heart that causes all the drag,
And you my friend, shall be the incorruptible trident.
However, in reality, there are no three, but only one.
The spirit of love and oneness is beyond time and form.

2. Neurochemistry 101
(Sonnet 2 - 4)

Sonnet 2

What is time, what is form,
It is all an illusion.
What has come, what has gone,
It is all an illusion.
No such thing as reality,
No such thing as truth,
It's all a trick of the mind,
It's all a hallucination most obtuse.
Role of reality is survival,
Role of perception is preservation.
All talk of truth is nonsense,
All sense of wisdom is self-gratification.
So forget about truth, wisdom and salvation.
Let's just make life a humane illusion.

Sonnet 3

The Biochemistry Sonnet

Chemicals breed prejudice,
Chemicals breed love.
Chemicals breed hate and rage,
Chemicals breed the atoning dove.
Chemicals breed walls of divide,
Chemicals breed the bridge to unite.
Chemicals breed death and disease,
In those very chemicals we find sight.
Chemicals are us, we are the chemicals,
In this mortal world there is nothing else.
While most are run by the whim of chemicals,
Some bend chemicals at will, as true sapiens.
Chemicals are the cause, chemicals are the result.
Awareness of chemicals is awareness of the world.

Sonnet 4

From dust we are born, in dust we'll merge,
The journey in-between must have some meaning.
If you have the will, then that's all you need,
To make a civilization out of air most thin.
There is not one but two universes,
One is real, another made up by our brain.
We live in the one that our brain has made,
And biases coax us to believe it as the only lane.
In this universe truth involves comfort not reason,
Assumption alone distinguishes right from wrong.
In such hallucinatory society stereotypes are archetypes,
And to question stereotypes is to bring ridicule along.
The human brain hasn't evolved to understand the universe.
If we must live in hallucination, let's make it a lover-verse.

3.   Fortune and Resources
(Sonnet 5 - 7)

Sonnet 5

In a world of indifference,
All inspiration is desperation.
In a world of apathy,
All capacity is desolation.
When the heart is blind,
The greatest of power is evil.
When the sight is tight,
Even a saintly one turns devil.
Real, unreal, all is in the neurons,
All of which is primed by nature.
We also hold the seed of expansion,
Which blooms when we defy selfish desire.
You see, puny minds make puny-verse,
Uni minds make uni-verse.

Sonnet 6 – Turkish

Aşksız Şöhret
(Bir Aşk Şiiri)

Seni çok seviyorum aşkım!
Bu itirafı duymak için ölüyorum ben.
Bunu neden türkçe konuşuyorum, biliyorsun!
Çünkü yağmurda ağlarsa, farketmezsin.
İngilizce söylersem herkes öğrenecek ki,
Ben sufi falan değil, sadece kayıp bir insanım.
Bu yüzden ben Şems'ın dilini konuşuyorum.
Benim gibi deliden korkacak hiçbir şey yok benim için.
Cok aciyor biliyormusun, bu yolculuk cok aciyor ama,
Dünyanın en güçlü insanı gibi davranmak mecburum.
Hala bazen tüm savaşlarımı unutmak istiyorum,
Bazen birinin kucağında kendimi kaybetmek istiyorum.
Sonunda sırrımı öğrendin, onurum artık sana emanettir.
Onu görürsen söyle ona, aşksız şöhret sadece lanettir.

Sonnet 6 - Spanish

Fortuna Sin Amor
(El Soneto)

¡Te quiero, te quiero mucho, mi amor!
Me muero por escuchar esta proclamación.
Estoy hablando en español, ¿sabes por qué?
Si lloras bajo la lluvia, no atraerás la atención.
Si hablo en inglés, todos descubrirán mi secreto,
Que no soy ningún sabio, solo un alma perdida.
Por eso hablo el idioma de la revolución,
Solo un amante loco puede entender a otro idiota.
Lastima mucho, este largo viaje lastima mucho pero,
Tengo que fingir que soy la persona más fuerte.
Todavía a veces solo quiero olvidar toda la guerra,
A veces solo quiero perderme en el abrazo de alguien.
Ahora sabes mi secreto - mi honor está confiado a ti.
Si la ves, díselo - fortuna sin amor es maldición para mi.

Note: I wrote sonnet 6 only in Turkish and Spanish, for it holds my secret which I don't want most to find out.

Sonnet 7

Sonnet of Human Resources

There is no blue collar, no white collar, just honor.
And honor is defined by character not collar.
There is no CEO, no janitor, just people.
Person's worth lies, not in background, but behavior.
Designation is reference to expertise, not existence.
Respect is earned through rightful action, not label.
Designation without humanity is resignation of humanity,
For all labels without love cause nothing but trouble.
The term human resources is a violation of human rights.
For it designates people as possession of a company.
Computers are resources, staplers are resources, but people,
Aren't resources, but the soul of all company and society.
I'm not saying, you oughta rephrase it all in a civilized way.
But at the very least, it's high time with hierarchy we do away.

Note: Call it skill resources, call it expertise resources,
but don't call it human resources. Because the term
'human resources' compares humans with commodity,
which is nothing but a new age slavery.

4.   Chunk of Uranium (Sonnet 8 - 10)

Sonnet 8

Fantasy and Responsibility
(The Sonnet)

Fantasy is good so long as it doesn't make us,
Oblivious to our responsibility of reality.
Imagination expands the mind for sure,
Only when it empowers our acts of accountability.
Growing up in India, I did not have superman,
But I did indulge religiously in some shaktimaan.
I don't know whether it influenced my making,
But it sure did fill my childhood with fascination.
People draw inspiration from different places,
That's a normal tenet of the mind, not a violation.
But inspiration is inspiration only when it leads,
To collective uplift, otherwise it's just delusion.
Fantasy is healthy when practiced with moderation.
Too much fiction paralyzes responsibility and reason.

Sonnet 9

The world doesn't need more avengers, but amantes.
Hear me well, my brave amantes, it's time to assemble!
More than Captain America we need Amelia Earhart,
More than Madame Web we need Madame Curie-like rebel.
Scrutinize all tradition with a fresh set of eyes,
Rebel against dogma, and stand up to discrimination.
Beliefs and doctrines surely have their place,
But none of it is above scrutiny of the new generation.
Each generation is to write their new set of laws,
Learning from the triumphs and downfalls of yesterday.
You just remember, that all roads lead to people,
And life that doesn't lift people is life gone astray.
Ayudar a la gente es la salvación de la mente.
Elevación de la gente es la elevación de la mente.

Sonnet 10

Each of us is a chunk of uranium,
Extremely unstable, but extremely potent.
Each of us is a chunk of alum,
Together we can clean up an entire ocean.
Divided we are dust, together we are a must,
Yet division is at which we're traditionally good.
Time has come to change that primeval habit,
Together we stand, divided we are screwed.
Once upon a golden age, is nothing but a myth,
Soon to be civilized, is also useless equally.
I believe, yes I do, only in the us and now,
I dream civilization as, once upon a soon to be.
Potential spent on perfection is potential gone awry.
Fall together, fly together, that's the way to life.

5. Who's The Idiot (Sonnet 11 - 13)

Sonnet 11

Ain't My Fourth of July
(The Sonnet)

Fourth of July comes and goes,
Yet slavery remains and thrives.
It kills in the name of supremacy,
It causes ruin in a pro-life guise.
Real advocates of life value life,
And place life above all belief.
Belief that values guns over person,
Is only pro-death and pro-disease.
Freedom involves accountability,
Without which we are just free animals.
Those who turn superstition into law,
Are no judge but a bunch of dumbbells.
This ain't my Fourth of July, for I actually value life.
Till all lives are deemed equal, I'll continue to strive.

Sonnet 12

Peygamber Parabrahma
(The Sonnet)

In a world where segregation is sanity,
True sanity begins with insanity.
You have to be insane to be egalitarian,
Inclusion is instilled through insanity.
In a world where indifference is sanity,
True sanity begins with insanity.
You have to be insane to take a stand,
Accountability comes through insanity.
In a world where selfishness is sanity,
True sanity begins with insanity.
You have to be insane to be wiped out for others,
Amidst inhumanity, humanity comes through insanity.
Sanity beyond sanity comes from the human beyond human.
Only such human is peygamber, such human is parabrahman.

Sonnet 13

I Am Idiot
(The Sonnet)

I am not as stupid as you think,
I am far more stupid than that.
My stupidity is beyond the grasp of,
All puny dreams of heaven and earth.
You have no idea how stupid I am,
To have an idea is to join the club.
What do the calculating snobs know,
Of the logic-defying madness of love!
The opposite of stupidity is narcissism,
I am the stupid beyond all such stupidity.
Where animals sell selfishness as sanity,
I am drunk, I am dumb, I am but humanity.
Better be a human and considered an idiot,
Than be a moron and worshipped as sage.

6. World Administrative Service
(Sonnet 14 - 16)

Sonnet 14

Messiahs don't drop from the sky,
As mortal suffering jumps the fence.
A messiah is just a mortal,
Minus all the indifference.
Peygambers don't jog down from jennet,
As people are troubled by malice.
A peygamber is just a regular person,
Who has conquered their prejudice.
Buddhas don't grow in a zen garden,
As the world reeks of bigotry.
A buddha is just an ordinary being,
Minus all the self-centricity.
Mind is the enemy, mind is the mate.
To all wounds of society mind is ointment.

Sonnet 15

World Administrative Service
(The Sonnet)

Awake, Arise, Oh Saint Soldiers,
Don't stop till you reach your goal!
Awake, Arise, Oh Saint Soldiers,
Don't stop till your dreams are whole!
Awake, Arise, Oh Saint Soldiers,
Don't stop till there is no injustice.
Awake, Arise, Oh Saint Soldiers,
Don't stop till the world is in peace.
Awake, Arise, Oh Saint Soldiers,
Do not stop till love is the only way.
Awake, Arise, Oh Saint Soldiers,
Don't stop till all prejudice is thrown away.
Civilization is born when all our sentience converge.
Puny minds make puny-verse, uni-minds make universe.

Note: Originally written in Turkish.

Sonnet 15 - Turkish

Uyan Be İnsan
(Dünya Hizmeti Şiir)

Uyan be insan, kalk be insan,
Amacına ulaşana kadar durma!
Uyan be insan, kalk be insan,
Hayaller gerçek olana kadar durma!
Uyan be insan, kalk be insan,
Her yerde adalet olana kadar durma.
Uyan be insan, kalk be insan,
Dünyaya barış gelene kadar durma.
Uyan be insan, kalk be insan,
Her yerde aşk olana kadar durma.
Uyan be insan, kalk be insan,
İnsanlar insan olana kadar durma.
Hadi kalk be kardeşim, bu dünya sana emanet.
Kendin için değil, insanlar için mücadele et.

Sonnet 15 - Spanish

¡Levántate Oh Luchador!
(El Soneto del Servicio Mundial)

Levántate oh luchador, adelante oh amador,
¡Hasta que alcances tu meta, no te pares!
Levántate oh luchador, adelante oh amador,
¡Hasta que hagas realidad tus sueños, no pares!
Levántate oh luchador, adelante oh amador,
Hasta que termine toda injusticia, no pares.
Levántate oh luchador, adelante oh amador,
Hasta que haya paz en la tierra, no te pares.
Levántate oh luchador, adelante oh amador,
Hasta que todos sean amantes, no te pares.
Levántate oh luchador, adelante oh amador,
Hasta que humanidad sea la realidad, no te pares.
Un nuevo mundo es la creación de nuevos humanos.
No lo olvides, la lucha de uno es la lucha de todos.

Sonnet 16

Humans and animals all are welcome in my house,
But not fundamentalists and nationalists.
Yesterday's nationalists were freedom fighters,
Today's nationalists are divisionists.
Even if you believe in fairies 'n spirits, you're welcome,
Even if you believe in angels 'n demons, you're welcome.
Even if you believe in frequency 'n vibrations, you're welcome,
So long as you don't practice hate and harm, you're welcome.
I am a human, and every human without hate is my family.
My heart is your home, no matter what your belief is.
But just like doctor and disease don't mix together,
Reformer and separatists are each other's antithesis.
I repeat, even the fiercest of animals is welcome in my home.
But there is no place for divisionism in this global dorm.

7.   Servant Scientist (Sonnet 17 - 19)

Sonnet 17

Genius By The Dozen
(A Sonnet)

Given the resources, I can build any technology,
Unlike some people, I do not need to hire genius.
Yet I gave up my obsession of electronics, because,
Building rockets is easy, building society not so much.
Not everybody is born with a silver spoon in mouth,
Rest of us have to choose among bread, dreams and tears.
But don't assume that I am whining about a misfortune,
Because, a reformer is worth a hundred entrepreneurs.
Rocket science is child's play for even a fisherman's son,
Cognitive Science is common sense for a laborer's child.
Yet you boast about a bunch of counterfeit geniuses whose,
Greatest power is that they are born with a golden hide.
If you seek true genius, lend a hand to developing nations.
And they'll give you Gates, Musks and Byrons by the dozens.

Sonnet 18

Servant Scientist
(The Sonnet)

No academician lent me a hand,
No industry gave an ounce of backup.
If I am what I am today, it's because,
I was too stubborn to give up.
Hence I can say without hesitation,
My legacy is built only by me,
Not an industry, not a benefactor,
And definitely not some university.
I come from the working class,
With neither education nor wealth.
Hence, my priority is always people,
Not comfort, nor intellect, nor gelt.
The name is Naskar, I'm a Servant Scientist,
Painkiller to people, pesticide to prejudice.

Sonnet 19

Live in the moment, not in the cloud.
Live amongst people, not in your phone.
Come to life to live the life,
Across all whining and shallow moan.
Humans ought to wear the clothes,
Yet today clothes wear the humans.
As per need humans may own the tech,
But no tech must own the humans.
The more you scroll the more you scream,
For social media feed is the modern casino.
If you think you can scroll off the hook,
You're already hurtling down the road to woe.
So I say, tech is supposed to lift you up.
If you're crippled by it, that's your own screw-up.

8.   Clicks, Impulse and Pieces
(Sonnet 20 - 22)

Sonnet 20

Click Less, Live More
(The Sonnet)

Moments are vessel for memories,
Don't waste them on snobbish hypes.
A memory cherished with a loved one,
Is worth more than a billion likes.
The less devices you have to charge,
The more charge you have for your mind.
The less you obsess over convenience,
The more you develop actual insight.
Purpose of camera is to capture memory,
Not to desecrate the moments seeking attention.
Purpose of a picture is to rejuvenate emotions,
Even a thousand pictures are useless without emotion.
Click less, live more - that is the motto of wellness.
Or else, click more, sick more - there is no treatment.

Sonnet 21

Couple days ago I had this impulse,
For buying some bluetooth earbuds.
Lo came, 'the less devices you have to charge,
The less your mind is cluttered'.
I have two devices, laptop and a phone,
That require daily electrical sustenance.
Any more, and it won't be a convenience,
But a damned nuisance!
Despite making simplicity my way of life,
Even I'm not infallible to the impulses of luxury.
But the difference is that I've trained my mind enough,
Not to succumb to frivolous cravings of material infidelity.
I am quite content with my 20 dollar shirt and two devices.
More devices you own, more your mind will be in pieces.

Sonnet 22

Sooner or later we all end up in pieces,
Life not in pieces is no life at all.
Make sure you're in pieces for the right reason,
Make sure it's not because of possessions but people.
Smart devices don't make a society progressive,
Intellect driven by arrogance and greed causes but regress.
What's needed is intellect soaked in the warmth of heart.
Societal coldness increases in proportion to smart devices.
Technology can be aid to life, but not the reason for living.
Logic is meant to empower life, not flood it with coldness.
Intellect is the greatest force of societal development,
But intellect not guided by heart is but fancy primitiveness.
Sooner or later we shall all end up six foot under.
Do you want your grave to smell of life or reek of blunder?

9.   The Uncultured Poet
(Sonnet 23 - 25)

Sonnet 23

Keyboard of Revolution
(The Sonnet)

I wrote most of my works,
On broken down laptops.
Perhaps that's why they work well,
With this broken down world.
I don't write to butter the assheads of pomposity,
My duty is to till the soil of grassroots reform.
That's why I feel at home creating on humble machines,
The very thought of fancy devices makes my stomach turn.
I once said to you, ripped jeans and twenty dollar shirt,
That's how we change the world, how we build the world.
Often a fancy exterior is indicative of a rotten interior,
It's a simple life that facilitates a magnificent world.
I don't need thousand dollar machines to cause ascension.
Give me a keyboard, I'll give you revolution.

Sonnet 24

Ethics and Songwriting
(The Sonnet)

I wish I could write music,
For one song is worth ten sonnets.
One sonnet is worth ten essays,
One essay is worth ten speeches.
That's why I have respect for those,
Singers who do their own writing.
While I pity the empty entertainers,
Who do nothing but counterfeiting.
It's okay if you sing someone's song,
At least make way for equal recognition.
Exploiting talent 'cause they're struggling,
Is fundamentally a human rights violation.
Every industry lacks ethics in its story of origin.
It's time we right the wrongs and get humanizing.

Sonnet 25

The Uncultured Poet
(A Sonnet)

There is a reason I never translate my works,
You can translate information but not sentiment.
So I carve humanity with not one but many tongues,
Yet due to alphabetical wall, much remain unspoken.
Human and culture must grow together in harmony,
All traditions of stagnation must be thrown away.
If a human can come forward across conditioning,
Why can't a culture do the same and meet halfway!
I sacrificed my language so I could feel you better,
Now I can't read the tongue of Tagore I was raised in.
Such an uncultured poet whose culture is the world,
Asks the cultures with borders just one little thing.
Take some lessons from Mustafa Kemal in modernizing.
A culture is enhanced, not diminished, by latinizing.

10. Language and Culture
(Sonnet 26 - 28)

Sonnet 26

Sonnet of Languages

Turkish is the language of love,
Spanish is the language of revolution.
Swedish is the language of resilience,
English is the language of translation.
Portuguese is the language of adventure,
German is the language of discipline.
French is the language of passion,
Italian is the language of cuisine.
With over 7000 languages in the world,
Handful of tongues fall short in a sonnet.
But you can rest assured of one thing,
Every language does something the very best.
Each language is profoundly unique in its own way.
When they come together, they light the human way.

Sonnet 27

Culture shapes the language,
Language shapes the culture.
When you absorb another language,
It reshapes your mental atmosphere.
Learning a language rewires the brain,
It expands our thoughts and emotions.
One small step towards a language,
Is one giant leap towards inclusion.
Language is a freeway to a culture,
It is a tangible way to becoming whole.
Come forward to adopt another tongue,
An entire culture will adopt you as their own.
English is okay, but plenty is lost in translation.
To gain a language is to gain insight into integration.

Sonnet 28

Human and culture are not two but one,
The way a human is, so is the culture.
But often the human alive forgets to be,
And ends up a photocopy of their ancestor.
Such stagnation is not the fault of culture,
It's the fault of the human without expansion.
One who cannot see beyond the rim of tradition,
Ends up another captive of the culture prison.
Culture expands only when the human expands,
How will it expand when human forgets to reason!
When the prison of history starts feeling cozy,
Nobody can rescue such people from degradation.
History serves best in pointing out to us the potholes.
Culture must come alive, instead of being a rotten mold.

11. My Faith is Humanity
(Sonnet 29 - 31)

Sonnet 29

A culture that doesn't evolve,
Is a pompei waiting to happen.
Either encourage expansion in society,
Or start digging grave for your children.
Even a flower cannot survive,
On last week's water, and,
You want a mind to survive,
On centuries old beliefs and opinion!
If this is not stupidity what is!
If this is sanity what is insanity!
Beliefs serving humans is good but,
Humans serving beliefs is a catastrophe.
So look back to see how far you've come,
But don't get stuck there, or else you're gone.

Sonnet 30

A human doesn't need culture to be good,
But every culture needs a human, to be good.
A human doesn't need religion to be good,
But every religion needs a human, to be good.
A human doesn't need philosophy to be good,
But philosophy needs a human, to be good.
A human doesn't need politics to be good,
But politics needs a human, to be good.
A human doesn't need science to be good,
But science needs a human, to be good.
A human doesn't need intellect to be good,
But intellect needs a human, to be good.
Goodness comes not from faith, culture or intellect.
Good and evil are but creation of the sapiens brain.

Sonnet 31

Dropout Scientist
(The Sonnet)

I am a scientist who doesn't have a degree,
I am a poet who has no control over words.
I am a philosopher who has no intellect whatsoever,
I am a monk with no idea, what it means to be religious.
If I am being honest, I have no clue what I am,
And I know quite well that you do not know either.
But believe you me my friend, one day in sheer awe,
Your descendants will come up with the rightful answer.
In my 30 years of life, I've traveled quite a distance,
Which will take the world at least a millennium to cover.
That's why archaic designations fall short to define life,
No designation is qualified to define a being beyond border.
My faith is humanity, my reason is humanity, my love is humanity.
I am but a glimpse of the future, without coldness and rigidity.

12. Facts and Fiction (Sonnet 32 - 34)

Sonnet 32

Coldness of reason is,
As dangerous as rigidity of faith.
Arrogance of knowledge is,
Far worse than absence of knowledge.
True knowledge makes us humble,
True reason brings understanding.
If there is no gentleness in life,
No reason can make life worth living.
To hell with faith, to hell with reason!
Without heart both cause disaster.
To hell with facts, to hell with fiction!
Without heart, both bring despair.
Love is to guide facts, love is to guide fiction.
If there is no love inside, we are just imitation.

Sonnet 33

We are not machines,
We can't live on facts alone.
To have a life worth living,
We must balance facts with fiction.
When you think of this with intellect,
It seems like a herculean task.
But lose the intellect and look with love,
And all of it will come like cake-walk.
Too much logic is lethal to life,
So is too little logic.
Too much fiction is lethal to life,
So is too little of it.
We need fiction, we need facts,
we need the whole works.
Let love lead you where it may,
all other leads are hogwash.

Sonnet 34

Until the entire earth is one nation,
There is no earth, there is no ascension.
Until all earthlings are one family,
There is no life, there is no liberation.
One earth, one humanity, is not only possible,
It is the only civilized way forward.
Till all the roots integrate into each other,
There's no way we can build a society just.
Justice is no affair of the law,
Peace is no matter of policy.
A being just builds a world just,
A world beyond sectarian identity.
Justice happens when civilians happen.
Peace happens when people happen.

13. All Peace is Fiction
(Sonnet 35 - 37)

Sonnet 35

Peace happens when people happen,
Light happens when life happens.
Truth happens when love happens,
Civilization happens when sapience happens.
Partisanism happens when politicians happen,
Ideologies happen when intellectuals happen.
Extremism happens when fundamentalists happen,
Terrorism happens when nationalists happen.
Deities happen when devotees happen,
Dictators happen when dociles happen.
Be no devotee to no figure, real or fiction,
And you won't end up a weapon of mass destruction.
War is but a mindless descendant of ideology.
The first step of warlessness lies across ideology.

Sonnet 36

Neuroscience of Ideology
(The Sonnet)

No matter the intention of origin,
No ideology can stand uncorrupt through time.
Even the perfect of theories fall apart, because,
The brain can't pledge obedience without being blind.
To maintain the grandeur of an ideology,
The mind chooses to switch off certain faculties.
Thus the mind starts digging its own grave,
As well as for the world, without even knowing it.
Ideology relevant today won't be relevant tomorrow,
But the ideology itself isn't aware of this.
Thus in the guise of savior it keeps raising sheep,
Who then turn defensive and ruin all possibility of peace.
Borders don't preserve peace, borders only breed war.
All peace is fiction till we treat every border
as Donald Trump's wall.

Sonnet 37

Outside The Museum
(The Sonnet)

Enough with, patria o muerte*!
Enough with, god save the queen!
Enough with, heil hitler!
Enough with, o say can you see!
Bronze age beings yell about national glory,
Stone age beings yell about religious glory.
Electric beings got no time for such make-believe,
On their shoulders walks the present of humanity.
There is no earth till all roots combine,
Till we crave for each other all roots are chains.
Museums add perspective on the direction of life,
But to spend a life in museum is life lost in vain.
Enough with vande mataram**,
it's time for vasudhaiva kutumbakam***.
To hell with nation, culture and tradition,
civilization awaits outside the museum.

(*homeland or death,
*hail the motherland, ***world is family)

78

14. Either Concubines or Civilians
(Sonnet 38 - 40)

Sonnet 38

Every Culture is My Culture
(The Sonnet)

If America fails in advancement, so will the world,
If South America fails in liberty, so will the world.
If Mexico fails in passion, so will the world,
If India fails in diversity, so will the world.
Every atom of planet earth is teeming with potential,
Yet most see nothing beyond the rim of their culture.
Culture is peddled in the world as a sectarian prison,
Yet the fact is, culture integrated is culture empowered.
Every culture belongs in every heart, every heart that is human,
While stoneage notions of culture still dominate the animal.
Simply put, till all cultures are ours, no culture is ours,
Any culture that claims supremacy belongs on a surgeon's table.
If humanity fails to embrace the strength of each culture,
There will be no humanity, there will be no culture.

Sonnet 39

Culture exclusive is a culture horribly sick,
Land sectarian is a land inhabited by skink.
Faith without some reason is but superstition,
World without integration is but a fancy clink.
Trading caves for concrete isn't progress,
Trading spears for shotgun isn't advancement.
Trading animism for dollarism isn't growth,
Trading cannibalism for nationalism isn't upliftment.
Dollars facilitate convenience, not character,
Medals don't make the mind, mettle does.
Beliefs exist to treat anxiety, not ignorance,
Parties only screw the world, not help it advance.
Enough with the possibilities drawn by materialists!
If my life isn't impossible, I don't wanna live.

Sonnet 40

Progress and partisanism don't go together,
Dollarism and sustainability don't go together.
Undisparity and materialism don't go together,
Secularism and superstition don't go together.
Celebrity and equality don't go together.
Morons make morons famous, snobs idolize snobs.
Sustainability and luxury don't go together.
Either you can have luxury or a disparity-free world
Nationalism and inclusivity don't go together,
Partisanism and peace don't go together.
Ideology and collectivity don't go together,
Narcissism and morality don't go together.
You have to decide, do you want to live as
ever-bickering concubines of pestilential politicians,
or as an undivided planet's undivided civilians?

15. Value of Tears (Sonnet 41 - 43)

Sonnet 41

Nueva Revolución
(El Soneto)

¡Viva la libertad!
¡Viva la revolución!
Pero, ¿qué es la libertad?
¿Qué es la revolución?
When no soul is discriminated,
That is liberty - es la liberación.
When no civilian is left unlifted,
That is revolution - es la revolución.
Revolution comes from the backbone,
of a person, not the barrel of a gun.
Necesitamos resolver injusticia sin revolver,
Este es el principio de la nueva revolución.
Stand up to each bullet con tu sonrisa valiente.
La respuesta a toda guerra es la gente.

Sonnet 42

Will you keep living as politicians' concubine,
While sipping fundamentalist moonshine,
Or will you wake up and take charge already,
To wipe out all megalomaniacal monkeyshine?
Politicians say jump, you jump without reasoning!
Nationalists say shoot, you shoot without thinking!
Fundamentalists say pray, you do so without question!
Transhumanists say obey, you go gaga without feeling!
Machines running the world is as stupid as pigs running it,
Cold logic is just as dangerous as mindless twattery.
Pledge allegiance to neither politicians nor technicians,
If you must take a pledge, pledge to lift up all humanity.
Road to a beautiful world doesn't go through a fancy freeway.
Road to a beautiful world goes through
the backbone of a human who doesn't walk away.

Sonnet 43

Even a thousand tongues fall short,
For a heart that has no ears.
Even a thousand philosophies fall apart,
If you don't fathom the value of tears.
One tear of joy caused by you,
Is worth more than a thousand accolades.
One tear of sorrow wiped by you,
Is a life lifted from the gloom-glades.
Be the glee to those in gloom,
Be gentle amidst the genteel.
Be the brave amongst the blue,
Be the knight amidst them who kneel.
Backbone by backbone the foundation is laid.
Heart by heart the soul of civilization is made.

16. Imagination & Inconvenience
(Sonnet 44 - 46)

Sonnet 44

Foundation of progress,
Isn't policy but people.
Bedrock of society,
Isn't beatitude but backbone.
The path doesn't make the feet,
It's the feet that make the path.
Feet that haven't trudged thorns,
Can't tell the world from the map.
Thorns make the pedestrian,
Roses make rosary.
Action builds the world,
Imagination treats anxiety.
Imagination that electrifies the feet is most righteous.
But the moment stagnation sets in,
all comfort must be crushed.

Sonnet 45

There is not one but two imaginations,
One brings comfort another extends horizon.
We need both for a healthy and cheery life,
A lot of horizon with a sprinkle of fiction.
Limit yourself to no horizon,
Today's horizon is tomorrow's history.
Perception is limited only by imagination,
With imaginative action there is no impossibility.
Make more use of the imagination of creativity,
Than the imagination that only brings comfort.
Revolution starts with inconvenient accountability,
There is no growth without discomfort.
To avoid inconvenience is to avoid development.
To chase comfort is to chase death and derangement.

Sonnet 46

A developing world is possible,
Only with a developing mind.
A reformed world starts,
Only with a reformed mind.
Beautiful music is possible,
Only with a beautiful heart.
Beautiful literature is possible,
Only with a beautiful heart.
Uplifting science is possible,
Only by the unarrogant.
Uplifting philosophy is possible,
Only by the unarrogant.
Clean mind creates clean society,
Not through puritanism, but
correction of prejudice and rigidity.

17. Cruelty, Arrogance, Judgment
(Sonnet 47 - 49)

Sonnet 47

Puritanism brings nothing but mindlessness,
Pursuit of perfection facilitates coldness.
Focus on self-correction not perfection,
Perfection brings but fancy primitiveness.
Somos la enfermedad, somos la cura.
Somos sensibilidad, somos locura.
We are the path where there is none.
Somos el camino, somos la música.
Somos el camino, somos comunidad,
Sociedad sin comunidad no es sociedad.
Con mente en la gente, con gente en la mente,
Nos levantaremos con la humanidad, por la humanidad.
Till we stop being a bunch of poncy, pretentious pillock,
Each obnoxious advancement will cause nothing but havoc.

Sonnet 48

Amidst cruelty arrogance has its role,
But you gotta tread with extreme caution.
Arrogance laid on the wrong person,
Is an appalling human rights violation.
Being brutal to avoid possible judgment,
Makes us a moron like those who judge.
Retaliating judgment with heartless cruelty,
Is not justice but primitive outburst.
Call out those who are pretentious,
Those who judge without understanding.
But let your response be guided by justice,
Observe well before you start accusing.
I repeat, arrogance laid on the innocent,
Can't be taken back with a million atonement.

Sonnet 49

If arrogance could eliminate judgment,
There wouldn't be any judgment left.
Humble on the inside, dinosaur on the outside,
What's needed is actually pretend arrogance.
When someone commits an injustice in front of you,
Ask them 3 times nicely to make amends.
If they still carry on like prehistoric pricks,
It's time for you to take charge as their parents.
We've been playing pretend justice for so long,
Each of us has turned into nothing but citizen vain.
It's the people who are to teach police what is law,
It's time to take law into our hands,
as unarmed and unyielding order incarnate.
Enough with the nonsense of delegation 'n representation!
A citizen off duty is a society of degradation.

18. Vanity, Education, Intellect
(Sonnet 50 - 52)

Sonnet 50

Citizen Vain
(The Sonnet)

All the law in the world cannot bring order,
In a society where the citizens are indifferent.
A citizen responsible is a society responsible,
A citizen on guard is a society with upliftment.
If the citizen can't tell right from wrong on their own,
It's not order but merely a revolting illusion of order.
Take away all punishment and you shall soon find out,
Law only forces repression, not reformation of disorder.
Without an actual reformation of the citizen's mind,
Sooner or later all nations end up in fundamentalist dump.
Pay less attention to law, and more attention to education,
Humanizing education is the only cure for the hoodlums.
In a world full of citizen vain, be a citizen vanguard!
There can be no order, unless the citizens stand on guard.

Sonnet 51

Education alone won't change anything,
First we gotta rid education of all archaism.
Rather than being a tool of indoctrination,
Education oughta be a force of undoctrination.
Education ought to be secular,
Education ought to be nonsectarian.
Sectarianism that passes as education,
Is the very antithesis of education.
Scriptures can be a part of education,
But they mustn't be the basis of education.
Cultures can be a part of education,
But they mustn't be the basis of education.
Any force that claims to liberate the mind,
Must first liberate itself from all divide.

Sonnet 52

Kindness is beyond the grasp of bookish intellect,
Otherwise, philosophers would be the kindest on earth.
Love is too grand to be explained by chemistry,
Or else, chemists would be the greatest lovers on earth.
Assimilation is too grand to be explained by reason,
Otherwise, scientists would be its purest specimens.
Harmony is beyond the grasp of textual theology,
Otherwise, theologians would be its foremost advocates.
It's more important to be kind than right,
It's more important to be kind than important.
Even a million pounds of belief is nothing,
In front of one ounce of kindness.
All of this can be realized by one person alone,
The one human being who has no sect of their own.

19. Competition and Failure
(Sonnet 53 - 55)

Sonnet 53

Real humans are attracted towards sectlessness,
Whereas animals have a knack for being sectarian.
Just like real men are attracted to strong women,
While shallow men want sheep for a woman.
Real men feel reassured when women take charge,
While pipsqueaks feel emasculated by the very thought.
Human beings feel empowered when others move ahead,
While dirtbags can't help but drag others down to rot.
Small minds try to feel big by means of condescension,
Human minds are those who live to lift the fallen.
Competition is but for race horses and night crawlers,
Society founded on competition is predisposed to degradation.
It's only the savages who boast about healthy competition.
Competition is but fodder for division and self-obsession.

Sonnet 54

A society where failure of one is success of another,
Is nothing but sick with pomposity fever.
A society where tragedy of one is triumph of another,
Is nothing but a glorified disaster.
A world where one seeks healing by shattering another,
Is nothing but a dimension of eternal despair.
Rotos juntos, curados juntos!
Broken together, woken together!
No sabes brokenness, no sabes liveliness.
Each wound holds the elixir of growth.
Wounds ain't obstruction, wounds are wind,
For the sails of your lifeboat.
Life is not the absence of wounds,
life is but the capacity of healing.
Wounds are ornament to the braveheart,
a heart that bites dust yet keeps walking.

Sonnet 55

Failure Reveals Friends
(The Sonnet)

When you try something new,
if you have someone to share it with,
Value that person more than the achievement.
Believe you me, it sucks to try new things,
When you got no one to share your excitement.
It's the people in our lives,
Who add value to our achievement.
This one time I thought I had found my rock,
But she got tired of my failures
and left me in bereavement.
All know about my triumphs, but till now,
I have no one to share my failures with.
It's easy to find people to share your success, but,
Very difficult to find one to share your struggles with.
Everybody will be there for you in the taking.
But nobody will be there for you in the making.

20. Life is Messy (Sonnet 56 - 58)

Sonnet 56

Don't look for someone you can talk sense with,
Find someone with whom you can talk nonsense.
Call it friendship, call it love, call it whatever,
Role of a companion isn't sensibility but acceptance.
That's why I walk around in shabby clothes,
That's how I get to know about people's true nature.
Everybody likes to butter up those in suits,
Those who smile at the people with nothing,
are the ones with real substance of character.
If you wanna find out who your enemies are,
Walk fancy and wait for the butter to pour in.
If you wanna find out the humans amongst the leeches,
Walk like a vagabond with your shirt not tucked in.
Be cautious of those who applaud your accomplishment.
And never lose those who walk by you in hopelessness.

Sonnet 57

We are the hope,
To those without any.
In a world run by apathy,
Let us be responsibly rowdy!
Helping those in need,
Is not charity, but humanity.
Responding hate with love,
Is not diplomacy, but divinity.
Magic and mysticism ain't divinity,
They are but prehistoric delusion.
When cruel, we are devil incarnate,
When kind, we are the supreme revolution.
To hell with passport - the world is our family!
And our family is our own responsibility.

Sonnet 57 – Spanish

Somos la esperanza,
Para los desesperanzados.
En un mundo de apatía,
¡Vamos, seamos desesperados!
Ayudar a los necesitados,
No es caridad, es humanidad.
Responder al odio con amor,
No es diplomacia, es divinidad.
Magia y misticismo,
No son divinidad, son ficción.
Cuando crueles, somos diablos,
Cuando amables, somos revolución.
El pueblo del mundo es nuestra familia,
Nuestra familia es nuestra responsabilidad.

Sonnet 58

Corazón amable es la iglesia suprema,
Corazón valiente es corazón de progreso.
Dirtless world begins with a dirtless heart,
Corazón con conciencia es el corazón del cambio.
All talk of change is nonsense,
If three forces are missing from the psyche.
Without conscience, courage and compassion,
All psyche is breeding ground for catastrophe.
Nothing about life is straightforward,
Life is messy - disaster one after another!
Only way we can survive this cataclysmic mess,
Is with extreme cruelty or unyielding character.
I choose the later, for cruelty is too big a burden.
Death with character has dignity,
without it, every breath is burden.

21. Errors and Shallowness
(Sonnet 59 - 61)

Sonnet 59

Without kindness,
Every breath is burden.
Without conscience,
Every thought is degradin'.
Without insight,
All courage is waste.
Without intention,
All talk is nonsense.
Without warmth,
All intellect is worm.
Without gentleness,
All progress is harm.
However, it is not wrong to make errors.
Wrong is the lack of corrective desire.

Sonnet 60

Errors and Evolution
(The Sonnet)

Elimination of error is elimination of evolution,
What's needed is correction of error not elimination.
Why you ask - because error expands perception,
While absence of error indicates absence of ascension.
Pebbles don't make mistakes, for pebbles have no life.
People make mistakes, for people are alive and kicking.
Make the error, mend the error, that is how we grow.
Don't be ashamed, don't be boastful, just keep correcting.
Those who never make mistakes, never amount to anything,
Failures are the foundation of a legend's legacy.
Let them celebrate your triumphs all they want,
You for one celebrate your mistakes and misery.
The shallow measure a person by their glorious victories.
Those with character measure a character by their tragedies.

Sonnet 61

The shallow's idea of character is shallowness,
The snob's idea of greatness is appearance.
The windbag's idea of capacity is charisma,
The egotist's idea of glory is selfishness.
Measure me not by how much I have gained,
Measure me if you must, by how much I've lost.
Look at not the light that I shine aloud,
Peek at the darkness that I hide from the world.
The world draws strength from my light,
I draw strength from my pain.
You only hear what I say with words,
If you wanna truly hear, hear me in the pouring rain.
When I am gone, don't go looking for my earthly base.
Look for my heartly base among the living sapiens.

22. Adopt The World (Sonnet 62 - 64)

Sonnet 62

Beauty captures the eye,
Behavior captures the soul.
Clothes facilitate shallowness,
Kindness conquers the world.
Focus on attachment, not arousal,
And you shall find your sweet everafter.
Focus on unification, not penetration,
And together you shall conquer all disaster.
But remember one thing, my friend,
You shall never receive love by begging.
Love got by begging isn't love but pity,
Which fades soon despite all the pumping.
Love is a lamp that the sane cannot get lit.
Partner is poetry that the sober cannot read.

Sonnet 63

Love is a lamp,
That the sane cannot light.
Peace is poetry,
That the sober cannot write.
Growth is green,
That the greedy cannot plant.
Insight is a state,
That the pompous cannot land.
Society is a cup of tea,
That the selfish cannot make.
World is a responsibility,
That the animals cannot take.
However, it's okay if the world feels too heavy.
Start by taking your neighborhood's responsibility.

Sonnet 64

Awake, arise and adopt the world!
You are the parent as well as heir.
Awake, arise and disrupt the divisions!
We the citizens are the world's caretaker.
If there is division, it's because of the citizens,
If there is oneness, it's because of the citizens.
State is a fiction that the citizens create,
Citizens are the truth that the state cannot fathom.
State is a dream, citizens are the dreamer.
The dream exists so long as the dreamer is asleep.
Civilization is the path, citizens are the pedestrian.
But the path doesn't exist if the pedestrian is asleep.
So I repeat - awake, arise, adopt the world!
Not of state, not of church, it's the citizens' world.

23. Enlightenment (Sonnet 65 - 67)

Sonnet 65

No state, better tomorrow.
No citizen, no tomorrow.
No church, better tomorrow.
No citizen, no tomorrow.
No politics, better tomorrow.
No civilian, no tomorrow.
No prejudice, better tomorrow.
No people, no tomorrow.
No head, lesser tomorrow.
No heart, no tomorrow.
No technology, difficult tomorrow.
No accountability, no tomorrow.
Though it feels, we the people are born of the world.
Truth is, world is born of people - no people, no world!

Sonnet 66

Seclusion Won't Do
(The Sonnet)

Each of you must turn into a sufi saint,
Each of you must turn into a latin lover.
Each of you must turn into a shaolin monk,
Each of you must turn into a bengal tiger.
It won't do to seclude yourself in a monastery,
It won't do to seclude yourself behind a desk.
The monk must come down to the streets of life,
The scholar must till the soil with their sweat.
Service of humanity is the fulfillment of divinity,
Service of humanity is the right use of intellect.
Occasional seclusion is good, to charge up the mind,
But life-long seclusion from society is sheer waste.
Enlightenment that doesn't eliminate separation
is no enlightenment.
Intelligence that doesn't elevate the collective
is no intelligence.

Sonnet 67

Transhumanism is Terrorism
(The Sonnet)

Intelligence comes easy, accountability not so much,
Yet intelligence is complex, accountability is simple.
Technology comes easy, transformation not so much,
Yet technology is complicated, transformation is simple.
In olden days there were just nutters of fundamentalism,
Today there are nutters of nationalism and transhumanism.
Some are obsessed with land, others with digital avatars,
While humanity battles age-old crises like starvationism.
When too much logic, coldness and pomposity set in,
Common sense humanity goes out of the window.
Once upon a time religion was the opium of all people,
Today transhumanism and singularity are opium of the shallow.
To replace the sky god with a computer god isn't advancement.
Real advancement is when nobody suffers
from scarcity of sustenance.

Note: Transhumanism is terrorism, for it is the very antithesis of life. Wasting precious resources on a pompous, narcissistic and megalomaniacal dream of extending life through cold, mechanical means, instead of helping to improve genuine human condition, transhumanists act as modern day terrorists who desecrate the very spirit of life and liberty without ever being held accountable. Let me tell you as a brain scientist and a computer engineering dropout - transhumanism is to brain computer interface (BCI), what nuclear weapons are to nuclear physics.

24. Head, Heart, Imperfection
(Sonnet 68 - 70)

Sonnet 68

Think with your head, act with your heart.
Bring them together, you'll conquer the world.
But before all else, get your priorities straight.
Without responsibility, we are all bag of dirt.
Pledge your allegiance to neither machine nor tradition,
Pledge your allegiance to neither facts nor fiction.
Embrace the good from everyone and everything,
Then use them in your own way for collective ascension.
A great leader is a sponge with filter,
Observes everything, but obeys nothing.
Keep your head and heart both wide open,
Let the whiff of wholeness rush all in.
Every atom in the world is teeming with lessons,
But no atom is free from biases and predispositions.

Sonnet 69

If I give in to one ist,
I'll have to give in to many more.
So no, I'm no feminist, yet I can shout,
Mujer-es cambio, mujer-es el mundo.
You don't need an ism,
To stand up for equality.
You don't need an ism,
To be catalyst of causality.
Many call me humanist, but,
Those who know me know I am not.
To me all designations, save human,
Feel nothing but an insult.
The human knows right and wrong without all the ism.
Leave your ism at the door, before entering my realm.

Sonnet 70

Keep your ism if you must,
But don't thrust it on another.
Keep your scripture if you must,
But don't impose it on another.
All scriptures are flawed,
All isms are imperfect.
If you still don't see it,
That right there is the problem.
Imperfection is life,
Imperfection causes ascension.
We grow through imperfection,
Not through perfection.
But all this is possible only when,
We acknowledge, then work on the imperfection.

25. Biases and Biology
(Sonnet 71 - 73)

Sonnet 71

There is nothing perfect about organic life,
We are all but imperfection incarnate.
If you want perfection read some fiction,
Life is messy, unpredictable and obstinate.
Yet if you can walk through the mess,
With your heart open and head held high,
You shall be worthy of designation human,
And you shall graduate from lifetown high.
The only secret to life is that there is no secret.
We pretend to be perfect, but inside we're all broken.
To embrace brokenness is to conquer brokenness,
Wound embraced is wound turned to ointment.
There's nothing perfect about human life, nothing ideal!
To embrace imperfection is human, to deny it is animal.

Sonnet 72

It takes a human to admit they are animal,
While the animal identifies as human without question.
It takes a human to admit they reek of biases,
While the animal feels beyond reproach and inclination.
A mind that is responsible for society, wants to grow,
While those self-absorbed stagnate in convenience.
When society flows through the veins like lifeblood,
No bias has power enough to impede the sapiens.
The world is coursing through my blood,
I can live without myself, but not the world.
You can take me away from the society,
But how will you take the society away from my blood!
Biases only control those who suffer from clinical moronity.
But they have no hold over the ones who burn for the society.

Sonnet 73

Reformers are too rowdy,
To be ruled by biases.
Lose the self among the people,
And you nip the bud of all biases.
Biases are biologically programmed,
To aid self-preservation.
Where there is no self to begin with,
There is no rule of predisposition.
Biology has an evolutionary predisposition,
Of narcissism, materialism and selfishness.
It also holds the underdeveloped brain-power,
Of humility, amity and kindheartedness.
Biology without selfishness is nothing but a myth.
But biology wasted on selfishness is a waste of heartbeat.

26. Control and Life (Sonnet 74 - 76)

Sonnet 74

We haven't yet manifested,
Our potential as biologic beings,
Yet we are obsessing over,
Turning into bionic beings!
We haven't leant to take care,
Of our very own home planet,
Yet we are headed already,
To ruin the red planet!
We haven't yet learnt to,
Transform our planetary home,
Yet we are boasting already about,
Becoming a interplanetary lifeform!
A species incapable of taking care of their home,
Will wreak nothing but havoc wherever they go.

Sonnet 75

Earth has plenty resources,
To suffice our need.
But no planet has enough,
Resources to suffice our greed.
Terraforming is easy,
Eraforming not so much.
Coding is easy,
Kindling not so much.
Soldering is easy,
Shouldering not so much.
Rocket science is easy,
Reform science not so much.
Rockets work on the principle of control.
To control a human is to lose all control.

Sonnet 76

Control is filth on the fabric of society.
Let's investigate it, shall we, my friend!
To control disease is called treatment,
To be aware of health is called wellness.
We crave for control because we want security,
Yet control never actually brings security.
It's in awareness that lies true security,
Only awareness brings actual, lasting serenity.
Peace comes when you befriend your pieces,
Strength comes when you befriend the weakness.
Insight comes when you acknowledge ignorance,
Life comes when you happily embrace death.
Where there is control there is no life.
Control repulses all love and light.

27. Helpers and Immortality
(Sonnet 77 - 79)

Sonnet 77

Love, light and life,
Are synonyms of each other.
Heart, human and humanity,
Are synonyms of each other.
Dignity, decency, determination,
Are synonyms of each other.
Character, conscience, compassion,
Are synonyms of each other.
Mind, mercy and mettle,
Are synonyms of each other.
Neighborhood, nation and world,
Are synonyms of each other.
Now let me tell you what really matters.
Self and society are synonyms of each other.

Sonnet 78

To shoulder the society,
Is to shoulder the self.
To shoulder the world,
Is to help oneself.
Every helper is human,
Every hoarder is animal.
Every lover is human,
Every avenger is animal.
Sacrifice is treasure,
Sacrifice is pleasure,
Sacrifice is measure,
Of a human, aka helper.
Helpers in every corner, helpers in every hood.
That's how we'll make the move, to reform from rude.

Sonnet 79

I have no intention of living just a few decades,
I must live forever or not at all.
And the only way we can live forever,
Is to give up this one life in lifting up the world.
I am immortality mad, have always been,
I even set out as a monk seeking it in divinity.
Then I realized, immortality is cosmic heirloom,
Of the mortal who is martyred for humanity.
Divinity is just a fancy name for everyday kindness.
Where there is kindness, there is divinity.
Human without kindness is human without humanity.
Serenity comes chasing when your sole concern is society.
Immortality is servant to the servant of humanity.
The day I took my last selfish breath,
was the beginning of my humanity.

28. Bless Me With Bullets
(Sonnet 80 - 82)

Sonnet 80

Why do we take breath,
Is it to stay alive!
Why do we eat bread,
Is it to stay alive!
Why do we drink water,
Is it to stay alive!
Why do we take naps,
Is it to stay alive!
Why do we look to mate,
Is it to stay alive!
Why do we have me time,
Is it to stay alive!
These just keep the body alive, nothing else.
The mind is alive when it lives beyond the self.

Sonnet 81

Bless Me With Bullets
(The Sonnet)

Just once let me die for the people,
Then I can live in peace.
Once I am wiped out for the world,
Then I can have my long awaited sleep.
Only when a bunch of bravehearts are sleepless,
Can the rest of humanity sleep in peace.
Only when a bunch of reformers are peaceless,
Will all the inequalities be appeased.
To hell with personal happiness!
To hell with the notion of personal and social!
There is no person, there is no planet,
Till the troubles of the world feel super personal.
Come all ye offended, charge at me
with your entire arsenal.
I won't resist, come and bless me,
with your bullets of denial.

Sonnet 82

I am a soldier, I am a reformer.
What will I do with a long life!
If you wanna bless me with something,
Bless me, O Nature, with courage to die with smile.
Life and death are civilian affair.
A reformer works each day with coffin in pocket.
There'll be no life for any of the civilians,
If the reformer slips into drunken enjoyment.
A reformer doesn't know what is a hangover,
Because a reformer is never sober.
Drunkenness of booze wears off in a day,
Drunkenness of sacrifice lasts through millennia.
The selfish drink to seek escape.
The reformer is too free to need such cheap help.

29. Grab The Cables (Sonnet 83 - 85)

Sonnet 83

Try booze, try bed,
Try the entire exciting lot.
Once you've appeased your curiosity,
It's time to focus on what's significant.
Inhumanity knows no vacation,
It won't wait while you recover from hangover.
It's okay to party on occasion but,
A life lost in booze and party, is utter disaster.
Greatest tragedy of life is a life wasted on self,
Greatest triumph of life is a life annihilated in help.
The secret to destiny is that there is no secret,
Destiny is but creation of the determined and persistent.
Awake, arise and grab the cables from your spinal cord!
A twenty watt brain can electrify the entire world.

Sonnet 84

Real study is that which,
Eliminates all separation,
That which helps us realize,
World and I are not two but one.
In a world where two are one,
Is a world with electricity.
Without oneness to charge the heart,
The world turns damp with inhumanity.
What's the use of all this separation!
Get rid of it all this very moment.
Vegetables thrive on separatism but,
Separatism is antithesis of sapiens.
To be human is to be undivided.
Divided human is forever unsapient.

Sonnet 85

Only the selfless are sapiens,
Rest are mere counterfeits.
Only the servants are the rulers,
Rest are just two-bit elites.
Only way to live is,
To live through sacrifice.
Only way to breathe is,
To breathe into others our own life.
O2 unshared isn't O2 but CO,
Sipping CO for others I stand keen.
In lifting another's terrible pain,
To breathe sarin even is super serene.
Trees are the greatest teachers on reformation.
Breathe in poison like a tree,
causing nothing but rejuvenation.

30. Most Wanted Mutation
(Sonnet 86 - 88)

Sonnet 86

In a world where most,
Are but effect of a system,
Stand alone and be the cause,
Of fearless rejuvenation.
In a world where the apes,
Are manipulated by illusive security,
Stand alone as anomaly,
And defy all who peddle security.
In biology it's mutation, in society it's anomaly,
Without which there is no ascension.
If life had rejected mutation 3 billion years ago,
We'd still be crawling around as single cell organism.
So I say, in a world where the law is self-centricity,
The mutation that is most needed is socio-centricity.

Sonnet 87

Don't confuse socio-centricity,
With obedience to society.
For that would be no different,
From today's society.
Treat the society like your children,
And you would know how to behave.
What you mustn't be is a spoilt brat,
And defy the society for the sake of defiance.
Revolution is a part of reformation,
But it is neither the cause nor purpose.
Defy the society's primitive habits,
Like a parent denies a child's wishes absurd.
Society doesn't know what's best for itself,
If it did, partisanists and fundamentalists wouldn't
have been able to keep the world divided.
It's up to the reformers to right the wrongs
and unite the planet.

Sonnet 88

The terrorist is a radical,
So is the reformer standing on duty.
But while the terrorist wants an exclusive society,
The reformer builds an inclusive society.
The billionaire is a radical,
So is the reformer with accountability.
But while the billionaire wants a society of elites,
The reformer builds a society without disparity.
The intellectualist is a radical,
So is the reformer awake with humanity.
While the intellectualist wants a society of logic,
The reformer builds a society of magnanimity.
There is no scope for change without being radical.
It's intention that distinguishes
human change from animal.

31. Greed and Autocracy
(Sonnet 89 - 91)

Sonnet 89

One bread can feed ten people,
If there is intention.
If there is no intention,
Billions fall short for the greed of one.
When there is intention 44 billion,
Can help end great many disparities.
But the absence of it makes a jackass,
Spread the tentacles of autocracy.
Alien are not those,
Who are not born of this planet.
Alien are those traitors who,
Don't give a fudge about the people of this planet.
Where there is intention there is ascension.
Absence of intention is facilitation of dehumanization.

Sonnet 90

No wonder they are trying to colonize Mars!
Warmth of humans repels cold blooded creatures.
Existence of billionaires implies not economic growth,
It indicates a crisis-ridden state
of disparity and violations.
The world needs hands of humanness,
Not tentacles of authoritarianism.
The world needs the madness to make billions smile,
Not the mad pursuit of billionairism.
And what the billionaires need is spanking up the khyber,
Since their parents failed to instill inclusivity.
When a child makes mistake, the parent must take charge,
The civilians must take charge
when billionaires violate humanity.
No autocrat is stronger than the citizens of earth.
Whenever autocracy raises its fangs,
citizens must crush them to dirt.

Sonnet 91

Citizens are the alpha, citizens are the omega.
Whatever good is possible, it comes from the citizens.
Citizens are the creator, citizens are the ravager.
Citizens make the autocrats, citizens can crush them.
Citizens are the cause, citizens are the effect.
There is no destiny, only determination of the citizens.
Citizens are the worshipper, citizens are the worshipped.
There is no religion, only humanity of the citizens.
Citizens are the gospel, citizens are commandments.
When citizens command with conscience, corruption falls.
Citizens are the altar, citizens are the idol.
When the citizens come down to the streets, dictators fall.
Autocrats and dictators rule because the citizens allow it.
Once the citizens wake up from hibernation,
it's time for their last wish.

32. Dutybound (Sonnet 92 - 94)

Sonnet 92

Do not think that I am advocating for assassination.
Assassination is an easy way out for autocrats and dictators.
They must be stripped of power and kept alive as petty criminal.
Only then they'll serve as an example to the wannabe conquerors.

Until the autocrats, dick-tators, and self-serving bureaucrats,
Are rotting in prison for life, like some common criminal,
All talk of law and policy is actually hypocrisy,
All talk of development is sheer snobbery of the animal.

Nothing good is possible till the citizens act as citizens,
Instead of like spineless children of boneheaded overlords.
Until the citizens become the lords and ladies of planet earth,
Hypocrites will keep desecrating humanity as dickhead demigods.

Victimhood has its own comfort, hence so many demigods!
Until the victims erupt as volcano, there'll just be chaos.

Sonnet 93

Even the worst of animal,
Deserves to live.
But human that behaves animal,
Must be put on leash.
The first step of justice,
Is accountability.
Those who fail to be accountable,
Deserve neither justice nor liberty.
Liberty founded on exploitation,
Is a threat to all humanity.
If we can't defend liberty for all,
We are unworthy of our own liberty.
It is time we redefine the notion of dictator.
Each civilian must turn into a benevolent dictator.

Sonnet 94

So long as the precise letters of the law,
Are more important than justice,
There'll only be the illusion of order,
But no justice.
Only the citizens can bring lasting justice,
Law has absolutely nothing to do with it.
Justice is not the absence of injustice,
Justice is the presence of accountability.
It is wrong to utter 'law' and 'order' together,
The actual phrase oughta be 'law and disorder'.
The purpose of law is to prevent disorder,
And it's the citizens' duty to manifest order.
Law is there to enforce punishment,
that's why it's called law enforcement.
Civilians are meant to stand dutybound for order,
that's why it's called civic duty, my friend.

33. The Supreme Commander
(Sonnet 95 - 97)

Sonnet 95

The meek fear the law, and law fears the corrupt,
We have to surgically alter this very paradigm.
Law and the corrupt both must fear the meek,
That is the rightful democratic paradigm.

People fear terrorists, terrorists fear fundamentalists,
We have to surgically alter this very paradigm.
Terrorists and fundamentalists both will fear the people,
Once the people grow the humane guts to defy all divide.

Civilians fear bureaucrats, bureaucrats fear politicians,
We have to surgically alter this very paradigm.
Bureaucrats and politicians both shall fear civilians,
Once the civilians stop dancing to their cockeyed chimes.

Neither politician, nor bureaucrat, nor law,
not even some terrorist or fundamentalist divider,
It is the people's world,
and people are the supreme commander.

Sonnet 96

Kill the terrorists,
You postpone terrorism.
Jail the fundamentalists,
You end terrorism.
Sentence the corrupt,
You postpone corruption.
Empower the civilians,
You eliminate corruption.
Disband the soldiers,
You postpone war.
Rehabilitate the nationalists,
You put an end to war.
All wars are the people's fault.
If the people had some common sense,
Would they be swayed by the divisionist lot!

Sonnet 97

If you still think, you have no background,
To stand up to oppression,
I tell you, listen - to stand up to injustice,
You don't need background, all you need is backbone.
I have no brand, I have no background,
All I have is my burning backbone.
Even a brain can be fooled with enough charm,
But no manipulator can fool a backbone once honed.
So I say, more than your fancy brain,
Hone your backbone, o brave civilians!
Stem cells for social reform,
Come from the backbone of civilians.
The world is an anatomically accurate
reflection of the human body.
A crooked world is the result
of a spinally crooked anatomy.

34. Reclaim The Planet
(Sonnet 98 – 100)

Sonnet 98

Reclaim The Planet
(The Sonnet)

Monsters spread their tentacles,
Because the masters are asleep.
Puny hyenas rule the world,
When the tigers are asleep.
Enough with pleading, to hell with decency!
Monsters only understand the language of roar.
When the predator comes to feast on your family,
Will you happily make way for them to pleasure more?
Doesn't the thought boil your blood – good, it should!
It means that your backbone is still alive.
Now turn all your attention on your every pore,
Feel through your veins the surge of might.
No more pleading,
no more begging to be treated as humans!
It's time for the humans to reclaim the planet
from the inhumans!

Sonnet 99

Rise, revolt and roar out loud,
No more pleading in front of prejudice!
Breathe, burn and brave out loud,
No more bearing in front of malice!

Dream, dare and dance out loud,
No more dangling as docile doormat!
Heave, hold and help out loud,
No more retreat in front of cold updraught!

Fall, fix and forge out loud,
No more settling as the forgotten figures!
Grow, glow, and break out loud,
No more groveling at the feet of bloodsuckers!

Only antidote to oppression is civilian unsubmission.
When the children go astray,
it's time for parental intervention.

Sonnet 100

The thin blue line is a state of mind,
So is the constitution, my friend.
Both serve the rich and the privileged,
Because the civilians take things for granted.
Until the civilians hail themselves,
Instead of the constitution, as vanguard of society,
Constitutions will remain playthings for the privileged,
Hence the very antithesis of democracy.
A constitution disloyal to the people,
Is just one more book that belongs in the dump.
A scripture that causes more division than unification,
Is the very definition of anti-religious scum.
No crown, no constitution,
no scripture, is higher than the people.
The moment they claim supreme rule,
it is time for the amantes to assemble.

BIBLIOGRAPHY

Archer M., (2000), Being Human: The Problem of Agency. Cambridge University Press.

Adolphs R (2003) Cognitive neuroscience of human social behaviour. Nature Rev Neurosci 4: 165–178.

Adolphs R, Tranel D, Damasio AR (2003) Dissociable neural systems for recognizing emotions. Brain Cogn 52: 61–69.

Andresen, Jensine, and Robert Forman, eds. Cognitive Models and Spiritual Maps. Bowling Green, Ohio: Imprint Academic, 2000.

Azari, Nina, Janpeter Nickel, Gilbert Wunderlich, Michael Niedeggen, Harald Hefter, Lutz Tellmann, Hans Herzog, Petra Stoerig, Dieter Birnbacher, and Rudiger Seitz. "Neural Correlates of Religious Experience."

European Journal of Neuroscience 13, no. 8 (2001)

Agar, N. (2004). Liberal eugenics: In defence of human enhancement. London: Blackwell Publishing.

Alteheld, N., Roessler, G., Vobig, M., & Walter, R. (2004). The retina implant new approach to a visual prosthesis. Biomedizinische Technik, 49(4), 99–103.

Antal, A., Nitsche, M. A., Kincses, T. Z., Kruse, W., Hoffmann, K. P., & Paulus, W. (2004a). Facilitation of visuo-motor learning by transcranial direct current stimulation of the motor and extrastriate visual areas in humans. European Journal of Neuroscience, 19(10), 2888–2892.

Bernstein R.J., (1971), Praxis and Action: Contemporary Philosophies of Human Activity. Philadelphia: University of Pennsylvania Press.

Bernstein R.J., (1976), The Restructuring Social and Political Thought.

Bernstein R.J., (1983), Beyond Relativism and Objectivism: Science, Hermeneutics, and Praxis. Philadelphia: University of Pennsylvania Press.

Bernstein R.J., (1986), Philosophical Profiles. Philadelphia: University of Pennsylvania Press.

Bernstein R.J., (1991), New Constellation. Cambridge: MIT Press.

Birkhead, T. R., Johnson, S. D. & Nettleship, D. N. (1985). Extra-pair matings and mate guarding in the common murre Uria aalge. - Anim. Behav. 33, p. 608-619.

Beauregard, Mario, and Vincent Paquette. "Neural Correlates of a Mystical Experience in Carmelite Nuns." Neuroscience Letters 405, no. 3 (2006)

Benson, Herbert. Timeless Healing: The Power and Biology of Belief. New York: Scribner, 1996

Bose, Subhas Chandra. An Indian Pilgrim: An Unfinished Autobiography, Oxford University Press, 1997

Bogen, J.E.(1995a), 'On the neurophysiology of consciousness: Part I. An overview', Consciousness and Cognition, 4.

Bogen, J.E. (1995b), 'On the neurophysiology of consciousness: Part II. Constraining the semantic problem', Consciousness and Cognition, 4.

Bremner, J. D., R. Soufer, et al. (2001). "Gender differences in cognitive and neural correlates of remembrance of emotional words." Psychopharmacol Bull 35 (3).

Brothers, L. (2002). The social brain: A project for integrating primate behavior and neurophysiology in a new domain. In J. T. Cacioppo et al. (Eds.), Foundations in neuroscience. Cambridge, MA: MIT Press.

Buss, D. D. (2003). Evolutionary Psychology: The New Science of Mind, 2nd ed. New York: Allyn & Bacon.

Buss, D. M. (1989). "Conflict between the sexes: Strategic interference and the evocation of anger and upset." J Pers Soc Psychol 56 (5).

Buss, D. M. (1995). "Psychological sex differences. Origins through sexual selection." Am Psychol 50 (3).

Buss, D. M., and D. P. Schmitt (1993). "Sexual strategies theory: An evolutionary perspective on human mating." Psychol Rev 100 (2).

Blakemore SJ, Decety J (2001) From the perception of action to the understanding of intention. Nature Rev Neurosci 2: 561.

Colapietro V., (1988), "Human Agency: The Habits of Our Being." Southern Journal of Philosophy, XXVI, 2, pp. 153-68.

Colapietro V., (1992), "Purpose, Power, and Agency." The Monist, 75, 4 (October) pp. 423-44.

Colapietro V., (2004a), "C. S. Peirce's Reclamation of Teleology." Nature in American Philosophy, ed. Jean De Groot (Washington, D.C.: Catholic University Press of America), pp. 88-108.

Carey DP, Perrett DI, Oram MW (1997) Recognizing, understanding and reproducing actions. In: Jeannerod M, Grafman J (eds) Handbook of neuropsychology. Vol. 11: Action and cognition. Elsevier, Amsterdam.

Carr L, Iacoboni M, Dubeau MC, Mazziotta JC, Lenzi GL (2003) Neural mechanisms of empathy in humans: a relay from neural systems for imitation to limbic areas. Proc Natl Acad Sci USA 100: 5497–5502.

Chomsky Noam, (2017) Requiem for the American Dream

Chomsky Noam, (2016) Who Rules the World?

Chomsky Noam, (2010) How the World Works

Churchland, P.S. (1986), Neurophilosophy (Cambridge, MA: The MIT Press).

Churchland, P.S. & Ramachandran, V.S. (1993), 'Filling in: Why Dennett is wrong', in Dennett and His Critics: Demystifying Mind, ed. B. Dahlbom (Oxford: Blackwell Scientific Press).

Churchland, P.S., Ramachandran, V.S. & Sejnowski, T.J. (1994), 'A critique of pure vision', in Large- scale Neuronal Theories of the Brain, ed. C. Koch & J.L. Davis (Cambridge, MA: The MIT Press).

Coyle EF. Integration of the physiological factors determining endurance performance ability. Exerc Sport Sci Rev. 1995;23:25–63.

Crick, F. (1994), The Astonishing Hypothesis: The Scientific Search for the Soul (New York: Simon and Schuster).

Crick, F. (1996), 'Visual perception: rivalry and consciousness', Nature, 379.

Crick, F. & Koch, C. (1992), 'The problem of consciousness', Scientific American, 267.

Damasio, A (2003a) Looking for Spinoza. Harcourt Inc. Damasio A (2003b) Feeling of emotion and the self. Ann NY Acad Sci 1001: 253–261.

d'Aquili, Eugene. "Senses of Reality in Science and Religion." Zygon 17, no 4 (1982)

d'Aquili, Eugene. "The Biopsychological Determinants of Religious Ritual Behavior." Zygon 10, no. 1 (1975)

d'Aquili, Eugene. "The Myth-Ritual Complex: A Biogenetic Structural Analysis." Zygon 18, no. 3 (1983)

d'Aquili, Eugene, and Andrew Newberg. The Mystical Mind: Probing the Biology of Religious Experience. Minneapolis: Fortress Press, 1999.

Daly DD. 1958. Ictal affect. Am J Psychiatry.

Damasio, A. (1994) Descartes' Error: Emotion, Reason and the Human Brain. New York, Putnams.

Damasio, A. (1999) The Feeling of What Happens: Body, Emotion and the Making of Consciousness. London, Heinemann.

Darwin, C. (1859) On the Origin of Species by Means of Natural Selection. London, Murray.

Darwin, C. (1871) The Descent of Man and Selection in Relation to Sex. London, John Murray.

Darwin, C. (1872) The Expression of the Emotions in Man and Animals. London, John Murray; also published 1965, Chicago, University of Chicago Press.

Dawkins, M.S. (1987) Minding and mattering. In C. Blakemore and S. Greenfield (eds) Mindwaves. Oxford, Blackwell, 151-60.

Dawkins, R. (1976) The Selfish Gene. Oxford, Oxford University Press; a new edition, with additional material, was published in 1989.

Di Pellegrino G, Fadiga L, Fogassi L, Gallese V, Rizzolatti G (1992) Understanding motor events: A neurophysiological study. Exp Brain Res 91: 176–80.

Deikman, A.J. (2000) A functional approach to mysticism. Journal of Consciousness Studies 7(11-12), 75-91.

Delmonte, M.M. (1987) Personality and meditation. In M. West (ed.) The Psychology of Meditation. Oxford, Clarendon Press, 118-32.

Dennett, D.C. (1988) Quining qualia. In A.J. Marcel and E. Bisiach (eds) Consciousness in Contemporary Science. Oxford, Oxford University Press, 42-77.

Dennett, D.C. (1991) Consciousness Explained. Boston, MA, and London, Little, Brown and Co.

Dennett, D.C. (1995a) Darwin's Dangerous Idea. London, Penguin.

Dennett, D.C. (1998b) Brainchildren: Essays on Designing Minds. Cambridge, MA, MIT Press.

Dewhurst, Kenneth, and A. W. Beard. "Sudden Religious Conversions in Temporal Lobe Epilepsy." British Journal of Psychiatry 117 (1970)

Dewhurst K, Beard AW. Sudden religious conversions in temporal lobe epilepsy. 1970 Epilepsy Behav 2003

Devinsky O, Lai G. Spirituality and religion in epilepsy. Epilepsy Behav 2008.

Devinsky, O., Morrell, MJ, Vogt, BA. (1995) 'Contribution of anterior cingulate cortex to behavior', Brain, 118.

E. Horvitz, "One Hundred Year Study on Artificial Intelligence: Reflections and Framing," ed: Stanford University, 2014.

Eckhart Meister, Selected Writings

Egidi R., ed. (1999), "Von Wright and 'Dante's Dream': Stages in a Philosophical Pilgrim's Progress", in

In Search of a New Humanism: the Philosophy of G.H. von Wright, ed. by R. Egidi, Kluwer, Dordrecht.

Fadiga L, Fogassi L, Pavesi G, Rizzolatti G (1995) Motor facilitation during action observation: a magnetic stimulation study. J Neurophysiol 73: 2608–2611.

Fogassi L, Gallese V, Fadiga L, Rizzolatti G (1998) Neurons responding to the sight of goal directed hand/arm actions in the parietal area PF (7b) of the macaque monkey. Soc Neurosci Abs 24:257.5.

Frith U, Frith CD (2003) Development and neurophysiology of mentalizing. Philos Trans R Soc Lond B Biol Sci 358: 459.

Farah, M.J. (1989), 'The neural basis of mental imagery', Trends in Neurosciences, 10.

Finlay BL, Darlington RB (1995) Linked regularities in the development and evolution of mammalian brains. Science 268.

Freud, S. "The Interpretation of Dreams", 1900

Freud, S. "Selected papers on hysteria and other psychoneuroses" Journal of Nervous and Mental Disease 1909.

Freud, S. "The Origin and Development of Psychoanalysis", 1910

Freud, S. "Psychopathology of everyday life", 1914

Freud, S. "Beyond the Pleasure Principle", 1920

Frith, C.D. & Dolan, R.J. (1997), 'Abnormal beliefs: Delusions and memory', Paper presented at the May, 1997, Harvard Conference on Memory and Belief.

Gay, Volney, ed. Neuroscience and Religion. Plymouth, UK: Lexington Books, 2009.

Gazzaniga, M. S. (1985). The social brain. New York: Basic Books.

Gazzaniga, M.S. (1993), 'Brain mechanisms and conscious experience', Ciba Foundation Symposium, 174.

Geschwind N. "Behavioural changes in temporal lobe epilepsy". Psychol Med. 1979.

Gellhorn, E., Kiely, W.F. "Mystical states of consciousness: neurophysiological and clinical aspects." J Nerv Ment Dis. 1972;154:399-405.

Gilbert SL, Dobyns WB, Lahn BT (2005) Genetic links between brain development and brain evolution. Nat Rev Genet 6.

Gray JA. The Psychology of Fear and Stress. 2nd ed. New York, NY: Cambridge University Press; 1988.

Gloor, P. (1992), 'Amygdala and temporal lobe epilepsy', in The Amygdala: Neurobiological Aspects of Emotion, Memory and Mental Dysfunction, ed J.P. Aggleton (New York: Wiley-Liss).

Greenspan, S. I. and S. G. Shanker (2004). The first idea: How symbols, language, and intelligence evolved from our early primate ancestors to modern humans. Cambridge, MA: Da Capo Press.

Grady, D. (1993), 'The vision thing: Mainly in the brain', Discover, June.

Gallagher HL, Frith CD (2003) Functional imaging of 'theory of mind'. Trends Cogn Sci 7: 77.

Gallese V, Fogassi L, Fadiga L, Rizzolatti G (2002) Action representation and the inferior parietal lobule. In: Prinz W, Hommel B (eds) Attention & Performance XIX. Common mechanisms in perception and action. Oxford University Press, Oxford.

Gallese V, Keysers C, Rizzolatti G (2004) A unifying view of the basis of social cognition. Trends Cogn Sci 8: 396–403.

Goldman AI, Sripada CS (2004) Simulationist models of face-based emotion recognition. Cognition 94: 193–213.

Grèzes J, Costes N, Decety J (1998) Top-down effect of strategy on the perception of human biological motion: a PET investigation. Cogn Neuropsychol 15: 553–582.

Grèzes J, Armony JL, Rowe J, Passingham RE (2003) Activations related to "mirror" and "canonical" neurones in the human brain: an fMRI study. Neuroimage 18: 928–937.

Gross CG, Rocha-Miranda CE, Bender DB (1972) Visual properties of neurons in the inferotemporal cortex of the macaque. J Neurophysiol 35: 96–111.

Guevara Che, The Motorcycle Diaries, 1992

Hari R, Forss N, Avikainen S, Kirveskari S, Salenius S, Rizzolatti G (1998) Activation of human primary motor cortex during action observation: a neuromagnetic study. Proc. Natl Acad Sci USA 95: 15061–15065.

Hardy, G. H. (1940). Ramanujan. Cambridge: Cambridge University Press.

Hall, Daniel, Keith Meador, and Harold Koenig. "Measuring Religiousness in Health Research: Review and Critique." Journal of Religion and Health 47, no. 2 (2008)

Harris, Sam, Jonas Kaplan, Ashley Curiel, Susan Bookheimer, Marco Iacoboni, and Mark Cohen. "The Neural Correlates of Religious and

Nonreligious Belief." PLoS One 4, no. 10 (October 1, 2009)

Halgren, E. (1992), 'Emotional neurophysiology of the amygdala within the context of human cognition', in The Amygdala: Neurobiological Aspects of Emotion, Memory and Mental Dysfunction, ed J.P. Aggleton (New York: Wiley-Liss).

Halligan PW, Fink GR, Marshal JC, Vallar G. 2003. Spatial cognition: evidence from visual neglect. Trends Cogn Sci.

Handbook of Emotions, Edited by Michael Lewis, Jeannette M. Haviland-Jones, and Lisa Feldman Barrett, The Guilford Press; 3rd edition (2010).

Hameroff, S.R. and Penrose, R. (1996) Conscious events as orchestrated space-time selections. Journal of Consciousness Studies 3(1), 36-53; also reprinted in J. Shear (ed.) (1997) Explaining Consciousness-The Hard

Problem. Cambridge, MA, MIT Press, 177-95.

Harding, D.E. (1961) On Having no Head: Zen and the Re-Discovery of the Obvious. London, Buddhist Society.

Hardy, A. (1979) The Spiritual Nature of Man: A Study of Contemporary Religious Experience. Oxford, Clarendon Press.

Harre, R. and Gillett, G. (1994) The Discursive Mind. Thousand Oaks, CA, Sage.

Haugeland, J. (ed.) (1997) Mind Design II: Philosophy, Psychology, Artificial Intelligence. Cambridge, MA, MIT Press.

Hauser, M.D. (2000) Wild Minds: What Animals Really Think. New York, Henry Holt and Co.; London, Penguin.

Hebb, D.O. (1949) The Organization of Behavior. New York, Wiley.

Helmholtz, H.L.F. von (1856-67) Treatise on Physiological Optics.

Hess, EH (1975) "The role of pupil size in communication," Scientific American, 233(5), 110–12.

Heyes, C.M. (1998) Theory of mind in nonhuman primates. Behavioral and Brain Sciences 21, 101-48; with commentaries.

Heyes, C.M. and Galef, B.G. (eds) (1996) Social Learning in Animals: The Roots of Culture. San Diego, CA, Academic Press.

Hilgard, E.R. (1986) Divided Consciousness: Multiple Controls in Human Thought and Action. New York, Wiley.

Hilton, E.N., Lundberg, T.R. Transgender Women in the Female Category of Sport: Perspectives on Testosterone Suppression and Performance Advantage. Sports Med 51, 199–214 (2021).

Hitler, Adolf. Mein Kampf, 1925

Hodgson, R. (1891) A case of double consciousness. Proceedings of the Society for Psychical Research 7, 221-58.

Hofstadter, D.R. and Dennett, D.C. (eds) (1981) The Mind's I: Fantasies and Reflections on Self and Soul. London, Penguin.

Holland, J. (ed.) (2001) Ecstasy: The Complete Guide: A Comprehensive Look at the Risks and Benefits of MDMA. Rochester, VT, Park Street Press.

Holmes, D.S. (1987) The influence of meditation versus rest on physiological arousal. In M. West (ed.) The Psychology of Meditation. Oxford, Clarendon Press, 81-103.

Holmstrom, David. 1992, Christian Science Monitor

Holt, J. (1999) Blindsight in debates about qualia. Journal of Consciousness Studies 6(5), 54-71.

Holloway RL (1996) Evolution of the human brain. In: Lock A, Peters CR (eds) Handbook of human symbolic evolution. Oxford University Press, Oxford

Iacoboni M, Woods RP, Brass M, Bekkering H, Mazziotta JC, Rizzolatti G (1999) Cortical mechanisms of human imitation. Science 286: 2526–2528.

Iacoboni M, Koski LM, Brass M, Bekkering H, Woods RP, Dubeau MC, Mazziotta JC, Rizzolatti G (2001) Reafferent copies of imitated actions in the right superior temporal cortex. Proc Natl Acad Sci USA 98: 13995–13999.

Jeannerod M (1988) The neural and behavioural organization of goal-directed movements. Clarendon Press, Oxford.

Johnson-Frey SH, Maloof FR, Newman-Norlund R, Farrer C, Inati S, Grafton ST (2003) Actions or hand-objects interactions? Human inferior frontal cortex and action observation. Neuron 39: 1053–1058.

Jackson, F. (1982) Epiphenomenal qualia. Philosophical Quarterly 32, 127-36.

James, W. (1890) The Principles of Psychology (2 volumes). London, Macmillan.

James, W. (1902) The Varieties of Religious Experience: A Study in Human Nature. New York and London, Longmans, Green and Co.

Jansen, K. (2001) Ketamine: Dreams and Realities. Sarasota, FL, Multidisciplinary Association for Psychedelic Studies.

Jay, M. (ed.) (1999) Artificial Paradises: A Drugs Reader. London, Penguin.

Jaynes, J. (1976) The Origin of Consciousness in the Breakdown of the Bicameral Mind. New York, Houghton Mifflin.

Johnson, M.K. and Raye, C.L. (1981) Reality monitoring. Psychological Review 88, 67-85.

Kadim I, Mahgoub O, Baqir S et al. (2015) Cultured meat from muscle stem cells: a review of challenges and prospects. J Integr Agr 14: 222–233

Kandel, E. R. In Search of Memory: The Emergence of a New Science of Mind, W. W. Norton & Company (2007).

Kandel E. R. Schwartz JH, Jessel TM. Principles of neural sciences. New York; McGraw Hill, 2000.

Kanwisher, N. (2001) Neural events and perceptual awareness. Cognition

79, 89-113; also reprinted inS. Dehaene (ed.) The Cognitive Neuroscience of Consciousness. Cambridge, MA, MIT Press, 89-113.

Karn, K. and Hayhoe, M. (2000) Memory representations guide targeting eye movements in a natural task. Visual Cognition 7, 673-703.

Kennedy, H., & Dehay, C. (1988). Functional implications of the anatomical organization of the callosal projections of visual areas V1 and V2 in the macaque monkey. Behav. Brain Res., 29, 225–236.

Kentridge, R.W. and Heywood, C.A. (1999) The status of blindsight. Journal of Consciousness Studies 6(5), 3-11.

Kihlstrom, J.F. (1996) Perception without awareness of what is perceived, learning without awareness of what is learned. In M. Velmans (ed.) The Science of Consciousness. London, Routledge, 23-46.

Kosslyn, S.M. (1980) Image and Mind. Cambridge, MA, Harvard University Press.

Kosslyn, S.M. (1988) Aspects of a cognitive neuroscience of mental imagery. Science 240, 1621-6.

Kinsbourne, M. (1995), 'The intralaminar thalamic nucleii', Consciousness and Cognition, 4.

Kjaer, Troels, Camilla Bertelsen, Paola Piccini, David Brooks, Jorgen Alving, and Hans Lou. "Increased Dopamine Tone during Meditation- Induced Change of Consciousness." Cognitive Brain Research 13, no. 2 (April 2002)

Kölmel HW. 1985. Complex visual hallucinations in the hemianopic field. J Neurol Neurosurg Psychiatry.

Koenig, Harold. "Research on Religion, Spirituality, and Mental Health: A Review." Canadian Journal of Psychiatry 54, no. 5 (May 2009)

Koenig, Harold, ed. Handbook of Religion and Mental Health. San Diego, CA: Academic Press, 1998

Kraepelin E. Psychiatry: A Textbook for Students and Physicians. New York, NY: Science History Publications; 1990.

Lauglin, Charles, John McManus, and Eugene d'Aquili. Brain, Symbol, and Experience. 2nd ed. New York: Columbia University Press, 1992

Lakoff, G. and M. Johnson (1999). Philosophy in the flesh. Basic Books: New York.

LeDoux, J. E. (1996). The emotional brain. New York: Simon & Schuster.

LeDoux, J.E. (1992), 'Emotion and the amygdala', in The Amygdala: Neurobiological Aspects of Emo- tion, Memory and Mental Dysfunction, ed J.P. Aggleton (New York: Wiley-Liss).

Levin, D.T. and Simons, D.J. (1997) Failure to detect changes to attended objects in motion pictures. Psychonomic Bulletin and Review 4, 501-6.

Levine,J. (1983) Materialism and qualia: the explanatory gap. Pacific Philosophical Quarterly 64, 354-61.

Levine,J. (2001) Purple Haze: The Puzzle of Consciousness. New York, Oxford University Press. Levine, S. (1979) A Gradual Awakening. New York, Doubleday.

Lewicki, P., Czyzewska, M. and Hoffman, H. (1987) Unconscious acquisition of complex procedural knowledge. Journal of Experimental Psychology: Learning, Memory and Cognition 13, 523-30.

Lewicki, P., Hill, T. and Bizot, E. (1988) Acquisition of procedural knowledge about a pattern of stimuli that cannot be articulated. Cognitive Psychology 20, 24-37.

Lewicki, P., Hill, T. and Czyzewska, M. (1992) Nonconscious acquisition of information. American Psychologist 47, 796-801.

Mesulam MM, Mufson EJ (1982) Insula of the old world monkey. III: Efferent cortical output and comments on function. J Comp Neurol 212: 38–52.

Naskar, Abhijit. "Homo: A Brief History of Consciousness", 2015

Naskar, Abhijit. "What is Mind?", 2016

Naskar, Abhijit. "Love, God & Neurons: Memoir of A Scientist who found himself by getting lost", 2016

Naskar, Abhijit. "Principia Humanitas", 2017

Naskar, Abhijit. "We Are All Black: A Treatise on Racism", 2017

Naskar, Abhijit. "Either Civilized or Phobic: A Treatise on Homosexuality", 2017

Naskar, Abhijit. "The Bengal Tigress: A Treatise on Gender Equality", 2017

Naskar, Abhijit. "Morality Absolute", 2017

Naskar, Abhijit. "Build Bridges not Walls: In the name of Americana", 2018

Naskar, Abhijit. "Fabric of Humanity", 2018

Naskar, Abhijit. "Citizens of Peace: Beyond the Savagery of Sovereignty", 2019

Naskar, Abhijit. "The Constitution of The United Peoples of Earth", 2019

Naskar, Abhijit. "Neurons Giveth, Neurons Taketh Away | Abhijit Naskar | TEDxIIMRanchi", 2019 https://www.youtube.com/watch?v=BNX-Q0ySm80

Naskar, Abhijit. "Mission Reality", 2019

Naskar, Abhijit. "Operation Justice: To Make A Society That Needs No Law", 2019

Naskar, Abhijit. "Every Generation Needs Caretakers: The Gospel of Patriotism", 2020

Naskar, Abhijit. "Hurricane Humans: Give me accountability, I'll give you peace", 2020

Naskar, Abhijit. "Revolution Indomable", 2020

Naskar, Abhijit. "Servitude is Sanctitude", 2020

Naskar, Abhijit. "Good Scientist: When Science and Service Combine", 2020

Newberg, Andrew. "How God Changes Your Brain: An Introduction to Jewish Neurotheology", CCAR Journal: The Reform Jewish Quarterly, Winter 2016.

Newberg, Andrew, and Stephanie Newberg. "A Neuropsychological Perspective on Spiritual Development." In Handbook of Spiritual Development in Childhood and Adolescence, edited by Eugene Roehlkepartain, Pamela King, Linda Wagener, and Peter Benson. London: Sage Publications, Inc., 2005

Newberg, Andrew. "The Neurotheology Link An Intersection Between Spirituality and Health", Alternative and Complimentary Therapies, Vol 21 No 1, February 2015.

Newberg, Andrew, Nancy Wintering, Dharma Khalsa, Hannah Roggenkamp, and Mark Waldman. "Meditation Effects on Cognitive Function and Cerebral Blood Flow in Subjects with Memory Loss: A Preliminary Study." Journal of Alzheimer's Disease 20, no. 2 (2010)

Nash, M. (1995), 'Glimpses of the mind', Time.

Nesse RM. Proximate and evolutionary studies of anxiety, stress and depression: synergy at the interface. Neurosci Biobehav Rev. 1999;23:895-903.

Nicolelis, Miguel. (2011) "Beyond Boundaries: The New Neuroscience of Connecting Brains with Machines--- and How It Will Change Our Lives", Times Books

O'Hara, K. and Scutt, T. (1996) There is no hard problem of consciousness. Journal of Consciousness Studies 3(4), 290-302, reprinted in J. Shear (ed.) (1997) Explaining Consciousness. Cambridge, MA, MIT Press, 69-82.

O'Regan, J.K. (1992) Solving the "real" mysteries of visual perception: the world as an outside memory. Canadian Journal of Psychology 46, 461-88.

O'Regan, J.K. and Noe, A. (2001) A sensorimotor account of vision and visual consciousness. Behavioral and Brain Sciences 24(5), 883-917.

O'Regan, J.K., Rensink, R.A. and Clark,].]. (1999) Change-blindness as a result of "mudsplashes." Nature 398, 34.

Ornstein, R.E. (1977) The Psychology of Consciousness (2nd edn). New York, Harcourt.

Ornstein, R.E. (1986) The Psychology of Consciousness (3rd edn). New York, Pehguin.

Ornstein, R.E. (1992) The Evolution of Consciousness. New York, Touchstone.

Penfield W, Faulk ME (1955) The insula: further observations on its function. Brain 78: 445– 470.

Penrose, R. (1994), Shadows of the Mind (Oxford: Oxford University Press).

Penrose, R. (1989), The Emperor's New Mind: Concerning Computers, Minds and The Laws of Physics (Oxford: Oxford University Press).

Persinger, "'I would kill in God's name' role of sex, weekly church attendance, report of a religious experience and limbic lability" Perceptual and Motor Skills 1997.

Persinger "Experimental simulation of the God experience" Neurotheology 2003.

Persinger, Corradini, Clement, Keaney, et al "Neurotheology and its convergence with neuroquantology" NeuroQuantology 2010.

Persinger, Koren and St-Pierre "The electromagnetic induction of mystical and altered states within the laboratory" Journal of Consciousness Exploration and Research 2010.

Persinger "Case report: A prototypical spontaneous 'sensed presence' of a sentient being and concomitant electroencephalographic activity in the clinical laboratory" Neurocase 2008.

Persinger and Saroka "Potential production of Hughlings Jackson's "parasitic consciousness" by physiologically-patterned weak transcerebral magnetic fields: QEEG and source localization" Epilepsy & Behavior 28 (2013).

Persinger. "The neuropsychiatry of paranormal experiences". J Neuropsychiatry Clin Neurosci 2001.

Persinger. "Neuropsychological bases of god beliefs", New York: Praeger, 1987

Persinger. "Temporal lobe epileptic signs and correlative behaviors displayed by normal populations", Journal of General Psychology, 1986

Perry BD, Pollard R. Homeostasis, stress, trauma, and adaptation. A neurodevelopmental view of childhood trauma. Child Adolesc Psychiatr Clin N Am. 1998;7:33.

Puce A, Perrett D (2003) Electrophysiological and brain imaging of biological motion. Philosoph Trans Royal Soc Lond, Series B, 358: 435–445.

Ramachandran VS. Behavioral and magnetoencephalographic correlates of plasticity in the adult human brain. Proc Natl Acad Sci USA 1993; 90: 10413–20.

Ramachandran VS. Phantom limbs, neglect syndromes, repressed memories, and Freudian psychology. Int Rev Neurobiol 1994; 37: 291–333.

Ramachandran VS. Plasticity and functional recovery in neurology. Clin Med 2005; 5: 368–73.

Ramachandran VS, Hirstein W. The perception of phantom limbs. The D. O. Hebb lecture. Brain 1998; 121: 1603–30.

Ramachandran VS, Rogers-Ramachandran D, Cobb S. Touching the phantom limb. Nature 1995; 377: 489–90.

Ramachandran VS, Rogers-Ramachandran D. Phantom limbs and neural plasticity. Arch Neurol 2000; 57: 317–20.

Ramachandran VS, Rogers-Ramachandran D. It's all done with mirrors. Sci Am Mind 2007; 18: 16–9.

Ramachandran VS, Rogers-Ramachandran D. Sensations referred to a patient's phantom arm from another subjects intact arm: perceptual correlates of mirror neurons. Med Hypotheses 2008; 70: 1233–4.

Ramachandran VS, Rogers-Ramachandran D, Stewart M. Perceptual correlates of massive cortical reorganization. Science 1992; 258: 1159–60.

Rizzolatti G, Craighero L (2004) The mirror-neuron system. Annu Rev Neurosci 27: 169–192.

Rizzolatti G, Fogassi L, Gallese V (2001) Neurophysiological mechanisms underlying the understanding and imitation of action. Nature Rev Neurosci 2:661–670.

Rock I, Victor J. Vision and touch: an experimentally created conflict between the two senses. Science 1964; 143: 594–6.

Rose´n B, Lundborg G. Training with a mirror in rehabilitation of the hand. Scand J Plast Reconstr Surg Hand Surg 2005; 39: 104–8.

Roberts, TA; Smalley, J; Ahrendt, D (December 2020). "Effect of gender affirming hormones on athletic performance in transwomen and transmen: implications for sporting organisations and legislators". British

Journal of Sports Medicine. 55 (11): 577–583

Royet JP, Plailly J, Delon-Martin C, Kareken DA, Segebarth C (2003) fMRI of emotional responses to odors: influence of hedonic valence and judgment, handedness, and gender. Neuroimage 20: 713–728.

Rozin R Haidt J and McCauley CR (2000) Disgust. In: Lewis M, Haviland-Jones JM (eds) Handbook of Emotion. 2nd Edition. Guilford Press, New York, pp 637–653.

Saxe R, Carey S, Kanwisher N (2004) Understanding other minds: linking developmental psychology and functional neuroimaging. Annu Rev Psychol 55: 87–124.

S. J. Russell and P. Norvig, Artificial intelligence: a modern approach (3rd edition): Prentice Hall, 2009.

Smith A (1759) The theory of moral sentiments (ed. 1976). Clarendon Press, Oxford.

Schilling, Vincent. 2017, indian country today

Stein, Stephen K. 2017, The Sea in World History: Exploration, Travel, and Trade

Simonsen R (2015) Eating for the future: veganism and the challenge of in vitro meat. In: Stapleton P, Byers A (Hg). Biopolitics and utopia. Palgrave Macmillan, New York (2015), S 167–190

Tesla N. "My Inventions", 1919

T. R. Society, "Machine learning: the power and promise of computers that learn by example," ed. The Royal Society, 2017.